Kadeja the Fulani Pearl Queen

Kadeja the Fulani Pearl Queen

Teacher's Resource material for the teaching of the Transatlantic Slave Trade

STELLA IFEYINWA OSAMMOR

Copyright © 2016 Stella Ifeyinwa Osammor
All rights reserved. No part of this publication may be reproduced, stored in a retrieval system or transmitted in any form or by any means , electronic, mechanical, photocopying , recording or otherwise, without the prior permission of the copyright holder.

ISBN-13: 9781904213468
ISBN-10: 1904213464

e-mail: delta.maria@btinternet.com

Printed and bounded in the USA by Createspace.

ELMINA CASTLE - GHANA

Elmina Prose

Culled from Silhouettes
of A Treasured Heritage

By Stella I. Osammor

Delta Maria Publishing House
1998 British Cataloguing

Lest History forget.
I whisper it on the wing of wind and time....
Every soul that left this shore was:
A Treasured Son.
A Treasured Spouse.
A Beloved Father.
A Revered Mum.
A Desired Daughter.
An adored Infant.

My walls still Reek with the Torment and Lament
of those left behind.
Here are anguished words of love, set on the wings
of wind and time.......
To all of my beloved.
Wherever they maybe.................

From Elmina: **THE BURNING HEART OF GOLD........**

One sunny day in Northern Ghana a bridal party set out on a long journey to Kumasi; the capital city of the Ashanti Kingdom. The bridal party stopped to sleep in Bedouin tents overnight. Kadeja the enchanting bride was full of joy and longed to be united to Kwesi her enchanting bridegroom. Kadeja's aunties asked Kadeja to share a tent with her cousins. The Bedouin tent was large and beautiful. The girls were tired from the journey but were still full of excitement as they settled down for the night.

Kadeja the Fulani Pearl Queen

The bridal party was very close to its destination. Although Kadeja was anxious to be united with her beloved spouse, Kwesi, she dreaded the thought of being separated from her kinfolk.

The wedding in Northern Ghana two months before had been grand. Her uncles and aunties had come from far and near for the wedding.

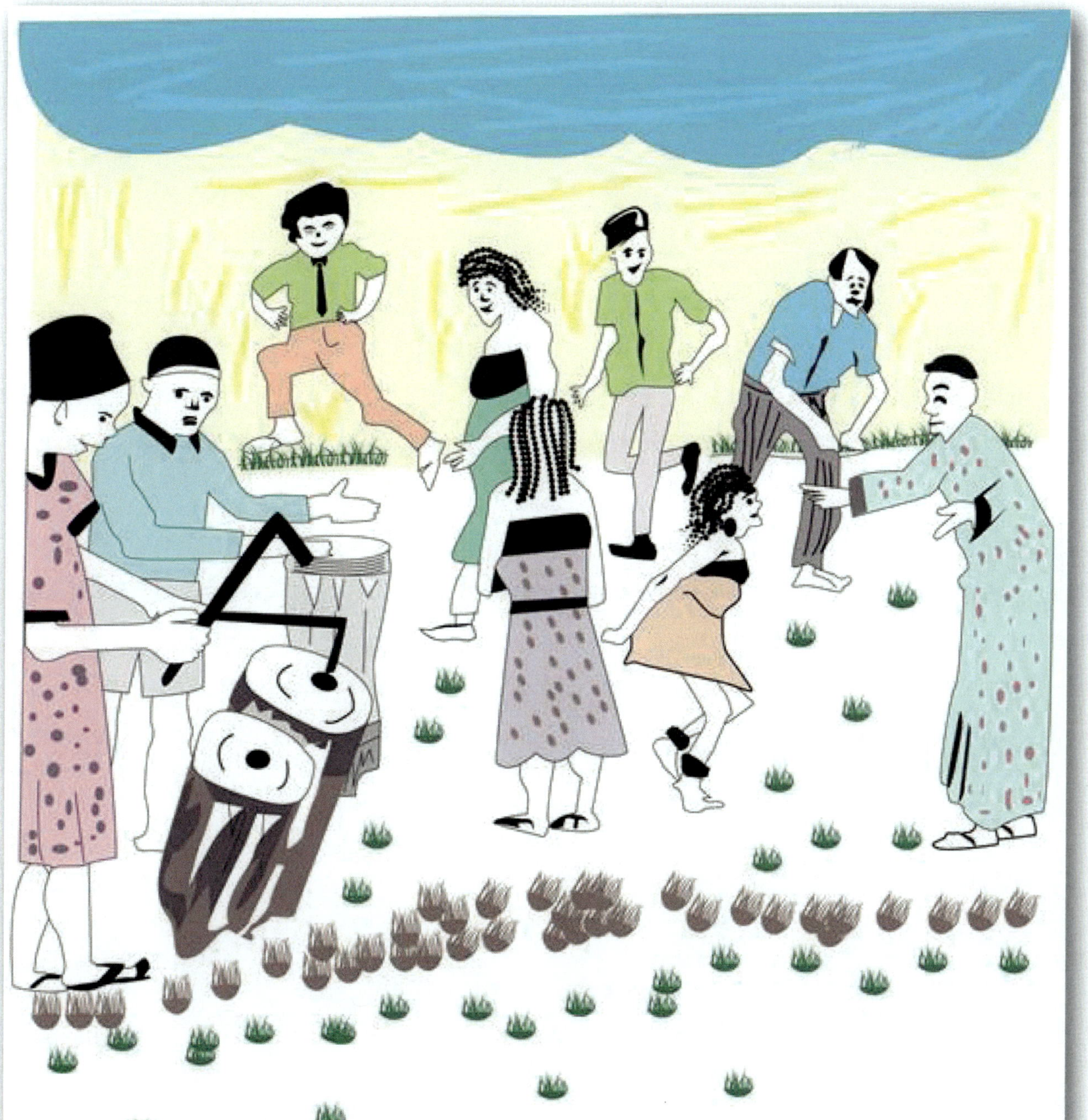

Kadeja's mother-inlaw was Fulani and her relatives from the Gambia and Mali had also attended the sumptuous wedding feast in Northern Ghana.

Several Ashanti Chiefs had accompanied Kwesi's father and uncles to the sumptuous feast in Northern Ghana. Kadeja's bride price had been 60 large horn bulls.

The adults in Kadeja and Kwesi's families negotiated about the bride price for several days. All throughout the negotiations, Kadeja prayed day and night to begin her new life with Kwesi…

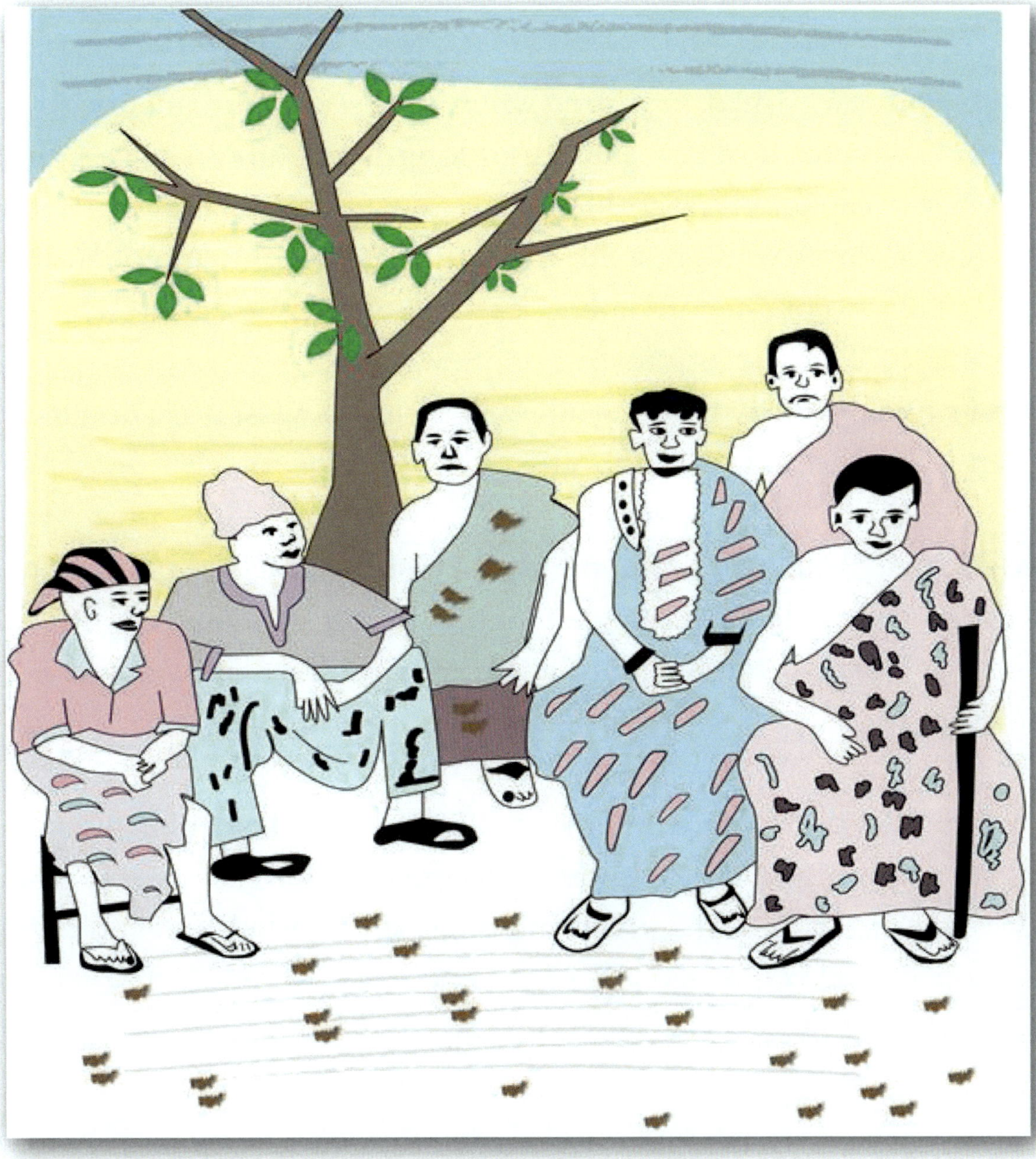

Kadeja and Kwesi had first met when Kwesi accompanied his uncle to Northern Ghana to purchase a hundred long-horned bulls for a grand feast in Kumasi, the capital of Ashanti land. Kwesi had been overawed by Kadeja's beauty. Kwesi stared at Kadeja intently with his mouth wide open. Kadeja's father Abubakare coughed in embarrassment and smiled as he whispered to Kwesi's uncle. "Please caution your nephew."

Kwesi's uncle angrily turned to Kwesi saying "Kwesi it is rude to stare at a maiden. Do you want to cause offence to these people?"

"He will learn." Abubakare said in a kind voice and carried on saying:

" Kadeja is our Fulani pearl queen. She is my last child and my only daughter. She was born to me in my old age. Her mother and I could never be parted from Kadeja. She is too precious to my kinfolk".

Nothing could stop Kwesi from staring at Kadeja, as the enchanting maiden served her father's guests refreshment. Kadeja felt Kwesi's eyes following all her movements. Kadeja's hands trembled as she handed Kwesi the gorge of clean water he had requested.

Kadeja the Fulani Pearl Queen

Kwesi drank the water thirstily and realised that his life would never be the same again. He would never forget the deep dark pools of Kadeja's eyes. His very soul seemed to have drowned in those eyes. Kadeja's necklace hung beautifully around her neck. Her skin was jet black, her dark gum contrasted sharply with her pearly white teeth.

Kadeja's fascinating presence lingered in the room long after she left.

Kwesi returned to Kumasi with his uncle in a daze. He was next in line to the Ashanti throne. He was a renowned warrior and was respected for his oratory, his wit, his fighting and hunting skills and his fearless courage. Kwesi was greatly loved by his kinfolk. He was their handsome strapping hero. Kwesi made his father the King extremely proud.

Kwesi had however become besotted with Kadeja and became increasingly despondent at the thought of never seeing her again.

Kwesi eventually went to his father and bared his heart to the king.

" I know my son " said the king. "You have an eye for beautiful Fulani women, just like I did many years ago, when I saw your mother and knew she had to be mine.

The King paused to think for some time and looked directly at Kwesi as he said with great determination: "I will send a delegation to Kadeja's father. Your mother's relations from Mali will accompany my brothers. They will persuade Kadeja's father to give you her hand in marriage" … …

It took seven delegations and several caskets of Ashanti Gold and bales of cotton cloth to convince Kadeja's kinfolk to give Kadeja to Kwesi in marriage.

Kwesi was beside himself with joy when on the seventh trip, Kadeja's father eventually agreed to give his blessing to the marriage. Abubakare was surrounded by his entire kinfolk as he spoke to Kwesi and his large delegation of uncles from Kumasi, Mali and the Gambia.

"Kwesi you have humbled yourself before me. You have exercised patience, perseverance and courage. We are fully persuaded that, you will cherish our beloved Kadeja. The wedding will take place 60 days from today. That will give our women time to prepare Kadeja for marriage, motherhood and her new home". Kwesi laid prostrate in gratitude before Kadeja's father and kinfolk. He returned to Kumasi with his uncles and began to make preparations for the wedding.

Kwesi built a beautiful mosaic house within the palace grounds for himself and his new bride.

Kadeja the Fulani Pearl Queen

The wedding of Kadeja and Kwesi in Northern Ghana was sumptuous. It lasted for 3 days.

At the end of the ceremony, Kwesi the bridegroom and his party returned to Kumasi to await the arrival of Kadeja his bride.

Kadeja travelled on horse-back with her beautiful bridesmaids.

She was accompanied by five aunts and some of her father's most trusted male servants.

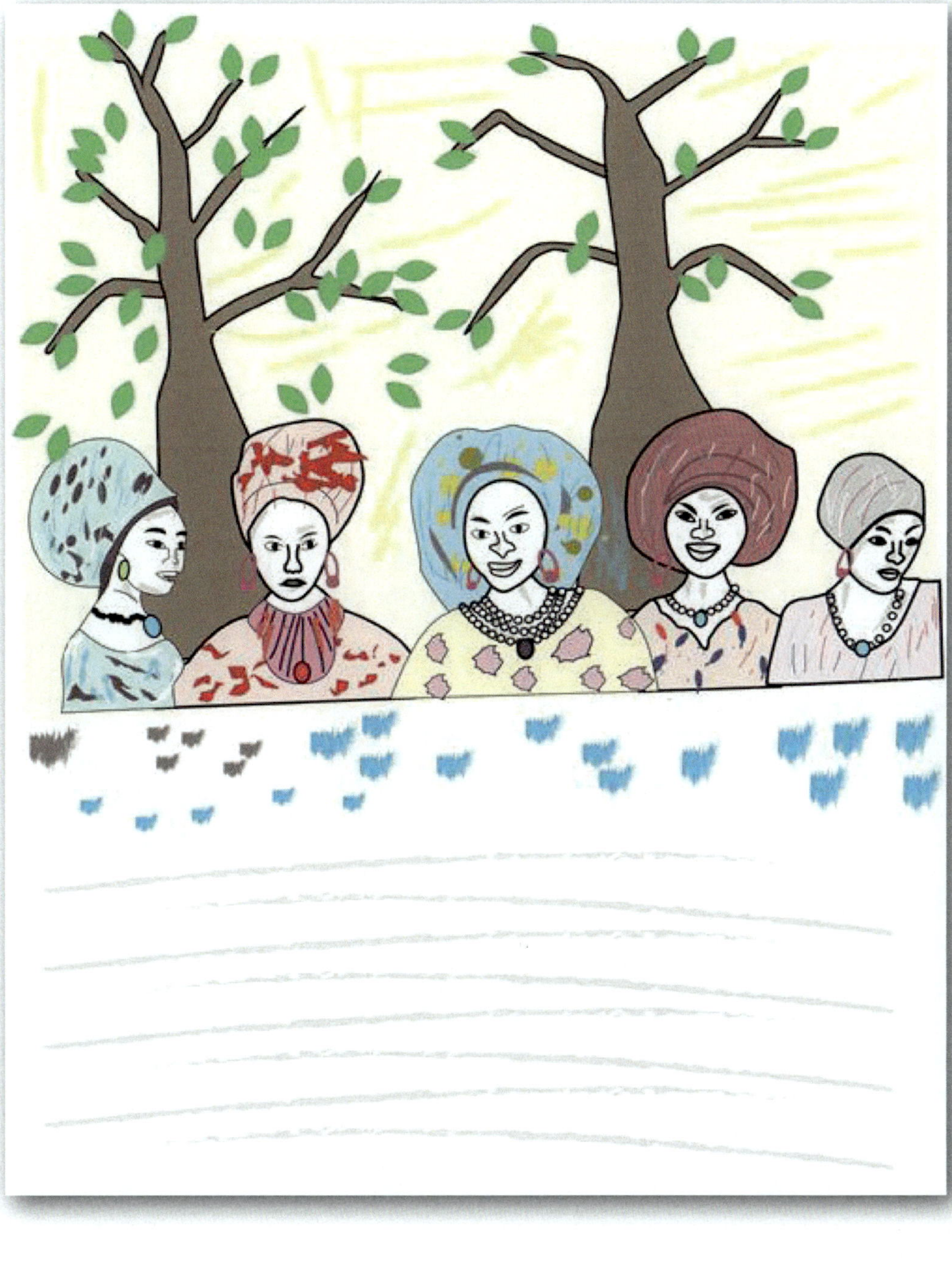

The bridal party set out for the long journey to Kumasi a week after the wedding. The party set out in the early hours of the morning. They hoped to arrive in Kumasi by early evening of the following day......

The journey was pleasant and everyone was full of good cheer. The bridal party was however glad when it arrived at Kumasi and began the ascent up the steep hill that would take them to the huge palace gates.

As the party approached the palace they heard cannons and gunfire ring out from the bushes to their right and to their left. Dogs ran out from the thick forest. Some women tore through the palace gates screaming: "Flee for your lives! Run! Do not go any further into Kumasi! Slave Raiders have set the palace on fire!" There was a stampede! Fire blazed out from the gatepost leading to the inner court of the palace.

Kadeja the Fulani Pearl Queen

Stella Ifeyinwa Osammor

The women who ran out from the building with blackened windows looked terrified and tried to get away from the palace and its surrounding with all their might.

White slave raiders began to fire at any man they saw. Some of the Fulani horsemen who accompanied the wedding party stabbed the slave raiders.

The fighting was bloody the dogs were ferocious and joined in the fight. Other slave raiders rounded the young women up, tied their hands behind their backs and stuck the nozzle of their guns into their backs. Kadeja and her cousins screamed with all of their might, because two of Kadeja's aunties lay dead on the forest ground.

The Fulani horsemen fought with all their might, but they were no match for the slave raiders' guns that kept shooting at people running from the flames, raging from the palace. Kwesi and hundreds of Ashanti warriors fought and rescued dozens of women and children from the grip of the ruthless slave raiders. Kadeja however was not among those the brave Ashanti warriors rescued. Kadeja and her cousins were taken to the dreaded Elmina Castle.

Kadeja tried to be brave, and to comfort her youngest cousin who had a bullet lodged between her shoulder-blade. Kadeja's cousin bled to death in the middle of the night. Kadeja herself slipped in and out of consciousness. Girls moaned in agony as that dreadful night turned to day. Kadeja was dazed and kept hoping that she would awake from her nightmare.

The next morning, a fierce battle broke forth in Elmina castle as Ashanti warriors stormed Elmina. The fierce fighting set a section of Elmina castle on fire. The battle raged from morning till early evening! Many of the Ashanti warriors were gunned down. Many slave raiders and dogs were killed by the brave warriors.

Kadeja the Fulani Pearl Queen

That very evening, Kadeja and her cousins were herded into a giant ship which took them away from the coast of Ghana into a new world from which Kadeja the Fulani pearl queen never returned……

Kadeja the Fulani Pearl Queen

ELMINA CASTLE (GHANA)

Elmina Prose

Culled from Silhouettes of A Treasured Heritage

By Stella I. Osammor

Delta Maria Publishing House
©1998 British Cataloguing

Lest History forget.
I whisper it on the wing of wind and time....
Every soul that left this shore was:
A Treasured Son.
A Treasured Spouse.
A Beloved Father.
A Revered Mum.
A Desired Daughter.
An adored Infant.
My walls still Reek with the Torment and Lament
of those left behind.
Here are anguished words of love, set on the wings
of wind and time.......
To all of my beloved.
Wherever they maybe...................

From Elmina: **THE BURNING HEART OF GOLD**........

Appendix page containing follow on work and comprehension questions on the story of Kadeja the Fulani Pearl Queen

Follow on work.
As follow on work, teachers could do the following:

1.) Show Pupils map of Ghana at the appendix page of the book
2.) Show pupils the location of Ashanti Land on the map
3.) Show pupils the image of Elmina Castle
4.) Show pupils the location of Kumasi in Ashanti land

COMPREHENSION QUESTIONS

1. How many of Kadeja's aunties got captured in the raid? Tick the correct box
   - ☐ 5
   - ☐ 3
   - ☐ 2
2. How many of Kadeja's aunties died? Tick the correct box.
   - ☐ 5
   - ☐ 3
   - ☐ 2
3. Apart from the use of guns, what else did the raiders use to capture the African people? Tick the correct boxes
   - ☐ Bows
   - ☐ Arrows
   - ☐ Guns
   - ☐ Dogs
   - ☐ Fire
4. What words could be used to describe the way Kadeja's parents must have felt?

5. What words could be used to describe the way Kwesi must have felt about the loss of Kadeja?
6. What words could be used to describe the way Kadeja must have felt?
7. The Transatlantic Slave Trade lasted for 3 centuries. How many years is this in total?
   ☐ 30 years
   ☐ 13 years
   ☐ 300 years
8. Elmina Castle was built by the Portuguese slave raiders. What is the name of the British member of Parliament who fought for many years to end the Slave Trade. Is it:
   ☐ Jacob Morris
   ☐ George Hope
   ☐ William Wilberforce
   William Wilberforce was life-long friend with a Nigerian man and fellow Slave Abolitionist. What was the name of Mr Wilberforce's friend (Tick the right box)
   ☐ Bola Brown
   ☐ Bola Bello
   ☐ Oludah Equono
   ☐ James Moses
9. What is the name of the leading Christian movement that fought for the abolition of the slave trade? Was it
   ☐ The Blowers
   ☐ The Corn People
   ☐ The Quakers

10. John Newton was Captain of a British ship which carried captured men and women from Africa to Britain and America in what was known as the Slave Triangle. John Newton wrote a song after he became a Christian and began a campaign against the evil trade in human beings. Was the song called
    ☐ I'm a believer
    ☐ Amazing Grace
    ☐ Jerusalem
11. What do you think is a Country's greatest wealth?
    ☐ Her Aeroplane
    ☐ Her Motorcars
    ☐ Her Men and Women
    ☐ Her Bicycles
12. How many Africans do you think were shipped away to Britain, Europe and America during the slave trade?
    ☐ Hundreds
    ☐ Thousands
    ☐ Tens of thousands
    ☐ Millions
13. Who were slave raiders most interested in capturing?
    ☐ The old men
    ☐ The old women
    ☐ The sick people
    ☐ The young men and women
14. Do you think the workforce of Africa suffered at this time?
    ☐ Yes
    ☐ No

15. Do you think Africa was able to develop properly during this time?
    ☐ Yes
    ☐ No

ELMINA CASTLE AS IT STILL STANDS IN GHANA.

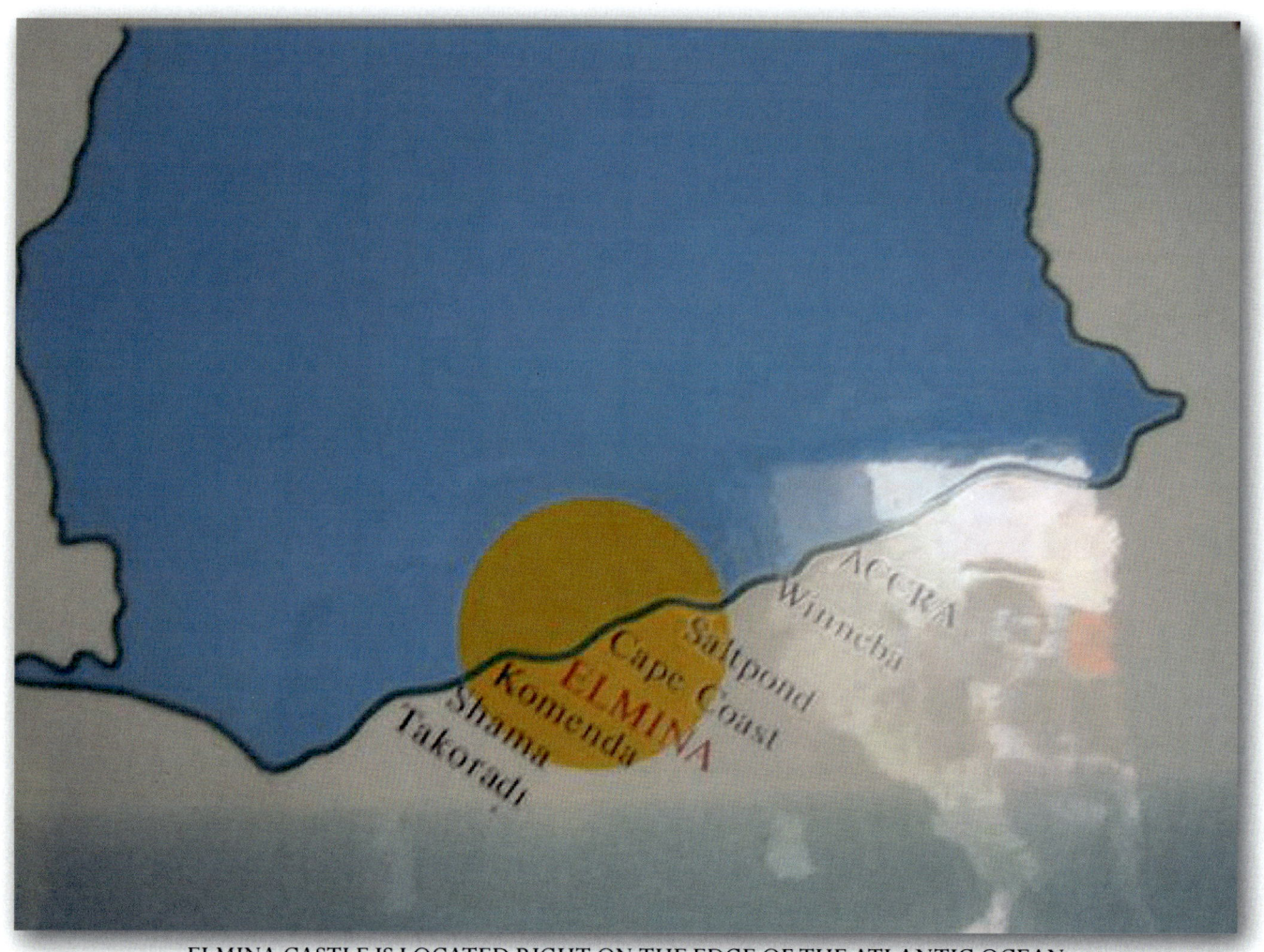

ELMINA CASTLE IS LOCATED RIGHT ON THE EDGE OF THE ATLANTIC OCEAN

A MAP OF PRESENT DAY GHANA.

GHANA CAN BE FOUND ON THE WEST COAST OF AFRICA

Appreciation:

I am grateful to God my father for giving me the enablement to give expression to the pain Africa felt and still feels at the loss of some of its strongest and brightest gems.

I thank Jimmy for his lovely illustrations.

I thank Seun for helping me with the technical challenges involved in realising this project

I thank Laraba for typing the manuscripts so patiently for us

I thank John for his never ending faith in me. Am grateful for your love…

Dedication

For black people everywhere who love Africa and call her "MOTHER"

Manufactured by Amazon.com
Columbia, SC
30 March 2017